30 DAY CONSECRATION TO ST JOSEPH

Fr Gerard Skinner

*All booklets are published
thanks to the generosity of the supporters
of the Catholic Truth Society*

CATHOLIC TRUTH SOCIETY

All biblical quotations are taken from the ESV translation,
except Psalms, which are from the Abbey Psalter.

Image on p. 13: Icon of St. Joseph in church of Abbazia di San Pietro
by unknown artist.

First published 2024
by The Incorporated Catholic Truth Society
42-46 Harleyford Road, London SE11 5AY.
Tel: 020 7640 0042. *www.ctsbooks.org*
© 2024 The Incorporated Catholic Truth Society.
All rights reserved.

ISBN 978 1 78469 773 0

Contents

Prepare the Soil of Your Heart. 5

Calendar of Possible Consecration Dates 7

The Apostles' Creed. 8

Litany of St Joseph. 9

Consecration Days 1-30 16

"Thirty Days" Prayer to St Joseph 106

Prayer of Consecration to St Joseph 109

Prepare the Soil of Your Heart

To consecrate oneself is a profound spiritual act. It is a simple act and yet a significant one. Words are used, but it is the heart that speaks to the heart of another. To consecrate oneself to St Joseph means turning to him with all one's heart to seek to become more like Jesus.

This consecration is of thirty days' length, resting on the tradition that St Joseph died just before Jesus began his public earthly ministry at the age of thirty.

St Joseph knows and loves the Saviour dearly, and he sees you and loves you as you prepare to consecrate yourself to him over thirty days. To prepare yourself for this month of devotion, it is good to begin by going to confession, so that the soil of your heart and mind may be weeded and tilled, watered by the grace of the sacrament and warmed by the sun of God's mercy, ready to receive such new seeds of life as God may grant to sow in you. If you are unable to make your confession before beginning the consecration, make sure you manage to do so within the thirty days, and certainly before making the final act of consecration on Day 30.

Jesus, Mary and Joseph were undoubtedly good neighbours in the places where they lived, looking out for the good of others. This should encourage you to decide upon some charitable deeds to carry out throughout the days of the consecration, as well as to ask for the grace of patience and a heart that desires to be forgiving. I suggest that you also commence the thirty days of consecration by professing your faith through the recital of the Apostles' Creed and by praying the Litany of St Joseph.

Before you begin each day's consecration prayers and readings, pause for a few moments to remind yourself that you are in the presence of God. Adore him. See St Joseph in your mind's eye, and simply say, "St Joseph, pray for me". Conclude every day with the *"Thirty Days" Prayer to St Joseph* on page 106, adding *the Prayer of Consecration to St Joseph* on page 109 on the last day. It is important to attend Mass on the day of consecration and say the act within a Church if possible.

Finally, the name 'Joseph' is rooted in the Hebrew '*Yosef*', meaning 'God shall add'. God shall 'increase' in the hearts of those who put their trust in him; God will 'enlarge' those faithful hearts. May this increase in grace be yours as you make this journey of prayer.

FR GERARD SKINNER

Calendar of Possible Consecration Dates

You can pray this consecration whenever you want and as many times as you want. Many people like to complete the consecration on a special feast day, depending upon their reasons for undertaking the consecration and the intentions for which they are praying. The chart below is to help you know when to start the consecration if you would like to finish on a particular feast day.

Start date	Feast day on which to finish	End date
25th December	Feast of the Holy Spouses	23rd Jan
4th January	Presentation of the Lord	2nd Feb
18th February*	Solemnity of St Joseph	19th Mar
2nd April	St Joseph the Worker	1st May
14th April	Our Lady of Fatima	13th May
19th July	Our Lady of Knock	17th Aug
3rd October	All Saints	1st Nov
11th November	Our Lady of Loreto	10th Dec
November**	Holy Family	Dec

*In a leap year, the consecration would begin on 19th February.

** The solemnity of the Holy Family usually falls on the first Sunday after Christmas. However, if Christmas is on a Sunday, it is best to check what day has been designated by your local bishop and begin your consecration twenty-nine days before the consecration date (which is Day 30).

The Apostles' Creed

I believe in God,
the Father almighty,
Creator of heaven and earth,
and in Jesus Christ, his only Son, our Lord,
who was conceived by the Holy Spirit,
born of the Virgin Mary,
suffered under Pontius Pilate,
was crucified, died and was buried;
he descended into hell;
on the third day he rose again from the dead;
he ascended into heaven,
and is seated at the right hand of God the
    Father almighty;
from there he will come to judge the living
    and the dead.
I believe in the Holy Spirit,
the holy catholic Church,
the communion of saints,
the forgiveness of sins,
the resurrection of the body,
and life everlasting. Amen.

Litany of St Joseph

Lord, have mercy on us
Lord, have mercy on us.

Christ, have mercy on us.
Christ, have mercy on us.

Lord, have mercy on us.
Lord, have mercy on us.

Christ, hear us.
Christ, graciously hear us.

God, the Father of Heaven,
have mercy on us.

God the Son, Redeemer
of the world,
have mercy on us.

God the Holy Spirit,
have mercy on us.

Holy Trinity, one God,
have mercy on us.

Holy Mary,
pray for us

St Joseph,
pray for us

Renowned offspring
of David,
pray for us

Light of Patriarchs,
pray for us

Spouse of the Mother
of God,
pray for us

Guardian of the Redeemer,
pray for us

Chaste guardian of
the Virgin,
pray for us

Foster father of the Son
of God,
pray for us

Diligent protector
of Christ,
pray for us

Servant of Christ,
pray for us

Minister of salvation,
pray for us

Head of the Holy Family,
pray for us

Joseph most just,
pray for us

Joseph most chaste,
pray for us

Joseph most prudent,
pray for us

Joseph most courageous,
pray for us

Joseph most obedient,
pray for us

Joseph most faithful,
pray for us

Mirror of patience,
pray for us

Lover of poverty,
pray for us

Model of workers,
pray for us

Glory of family life,
pray for us

Guardian of virgins,
pray for us

Pillar of families,
pray for us

Support in difficulties,
pray for us

Solace of the wretched,
pray for us

Hope of the sick,
pray for us

Patron of exiles,
pray for us

Patron of the afflicted,
pray for us

Patron of the poor,
pray for us

Patron of the dying,
pray for us

Terror of demons,
pray for us

Protector of Holy Church,
pray for us

Lamb of God, who takes away the sins of the world,
spare us, O Lord.

Lamb of God, who takes away the sins of the world,
graciously hear us, O Lord.

Lamb of God, who takes away the sins of the world,
have mercy on us, O Lord.

He made him the lord of his household,
and prince over all his possessions.

Let us pray:
O God, in your ineffable providence you were pleased to choose Blessed Joseph to be the spouse of your most holy Mother: grant, we beg you, that we may be worthy to have him for our intercessor in heaven whom on earth we venerate as our protector: You who live and reign for ever and ever. Amen.

[There is] a prayer to Saint Joseph to which I am particularly attached and which I have recited every day for more than forty years. It is a prayer that I found in a prayer book of the Sisters of Jesus and Mary, from the 1700s, the end of the 18th century. It is very beautiful, but more than a prayer it is a challenge, to this friend, to this father, to this our guardian, who is Saint Joseph. It would be wonderful if you could learn this prayer and repeat it. I will read it.

"Glorious Patriarch St Joseph, whose power makes the impossible possible, come to my aid in these times of anguish and difficulty. Take under your protection the serious and troubling situations that I commend to you, that they may have a happy outcome. My beloved father, all my trust is in you. Let it not be said that I invoked you in vain, and since you can do everything with Jesus and Mary, show me that your goodness is as great as your power."[1]

PORE FRANCIS

30 DAY
CONSECRATION TO
ST JOSEPH

Day 1 – Holy Trinity, One God

Theme: "…until Christ is formed in you." (*Ga* 4:19)

Opening Prayer

Remember, O most chaste spouse of the Virgin Mary, that never has it been known that anyone who asked for your help and sought your intercession was left unaided. Full of confidence in your power, I hasten to you, and beg your protection. Listen, O foster father of the Redeemer, to my humble prayer, and in your goodness hear and answer me. Amen.

Scripture

For this reason I bow my knees before the Father, from whom every family in heaven and on earth is named, that according to the riches of his glory he may grant you to be strengthened with power through his Spirit in your inner being, so that Christ may dwell in your hearts through faith – that you, being rooted and grounded in love, may have strength to comprehend with all the saints what is the breadth and length and height and depth, and to know the love of Christ that surpasses knowledge, that you may be filled with all the fullness of God. Now to him who is able to do far more abundantly than all that we ask or think, according to the power at work within us, to him be glory in the church and in Christ Jesus throughout all generations, for ever and ever. Amen. (*Ep* 3:14-21)

Reading from St John Henry Newman

When, for our sakes, the Son came on earth and took our flesh, yet he would not live without the sympathy of others. For thirty years he lived with Mary and Joseph and thus formed a shadow of the Heavenly Trinity on earth. O the perfection of that sympathy which existed between the three! Not a look of one, but the other two understood, as expressed, better than if expressed in a thousand words – nay more than understood, accepted, echoed, corroborated. It was like three instruments absolutely in tune which all vibrate when one vibrates, and vibrate either one and the same note, or in perfect harmony.[2]

Reflection

Through the intercession of St Joseph and by the power of the Holy Spirit, we hope and pray that the image of Christ, whom the saint so lovingly nurtured, will be restored in our hearts and minds and that our lives are pleasing to our heavenly Father. Let us ponder on the union with Christ that we enjoy through the Sacrament of Baptism when we became the adopted children of God, privileged to speak to him in prayer and to say, "Our Father".

Prayer of Pope St John XXIII

St Joseph, guardian of Jesus and chaste husband of
Mary, you passed your life in loving fulfilment of
duty. You supported the holy family of Nazareth with
the work of your hands. Kindly protect those who
trustingly come to you. You know their aspirations,
their hardships, their hopes. They look to you because
they know you will understand and protect them.
You too knew trial, labour and weariness. But amid
the worries of material life, your soul was full of deep
peace and sang out in true joy through intimacy with
God's Son entrusted to you and with Mary, his tender
Mother. Assure those you protect that they do not
labour alone. Teach them to find Jesus near them and
to watch over him faithfully as you have done. Amen.

Day 2 – Abraham, Our Father in Faith

Theme: Faith in God

Opening Prayer

Remember, O most chaste spouse of the Virgin Mary, that never has it been known that anyone who asked for your help and sought your intercession was left unaided. Full of confidence in your power, I hasten to you, and beg your protection. Listen, O foster father of the Redeemer, to my humble prayer, and in your goodness hear and answer me. Amen.

Scripture

For the promise to Abraham and his offspring that he would be heir of the world did not come through the law but through the righteousness of faith. That is why it depends on faith, in order that the promise may rest on grace and be guaranteed to all his offspring – not only to the adherent of the law but also to the one who shares the faith of Abraham, who is the father of us all, as it is written, "I have made you the father of many nations" – in the presence of the God in whom he believed, who gives life to the dead and calls into existence the things that do not exist. In hope he believed against hope, that he should become the father of many nations, as he had been told, "So shall your offspring be." That is why his faith was "counted to him as righteousness". (*Rm* 4:13, 16-18, 22)

Reading from Pope Benedict XVI

The Gospel of Matthew highlights in a special way the Messianic prophecies which reached fulfilment through the role that Joseph played: the birth of Jesus in Bethlehem (*Mt* 2:1-6); his journey through Egypt, where the Holy Family took refuge (*Mt* 2:13-15); the nickname, the "Nazarene" (*Mt* 2:22-23).

In all of this he showed himself, like his spouse Mary, an authentic heir of Abraham's faith: faith in God who guides the events of history according to his mysterious salvific plan. His greatness, like Mary's, stands out even more because his mission was carried out in the humility and hiddenness of the house of Nazareth. Moreover, God himself, in the person of his Incarnate Son, chose this way and style of life – humility and hiddenness – in his earthly existence.

From the example of St Joseph we all receive a strong invitation to carry out with fidelity, simplicity and modesty the task that Providence has entrusted to us.[3]

Reflection

"In hope he believed against hope". For both Abraham and St Joseph, their faith in God was greatly tested. They trusted, yet they hesitated, ultimately believing having first questioned. "We have believed, and have come to know," responded St Peter to Jesus in the Gospel of John (6:69) – to discern God's ways, to know him and begin to perceive his plan, we first need the eyes of faith. "I believe; help my unbelief!" (*Mk* 9:24).

Prayer

O Lord, we commend ourselves to St Joseph, the glorious Patriarch whom you chose as the head of the Holy Family and the patron and protector of the whole Church. Trusting in the power of his intercession in heaven, we entrust especially to you our families and all our intentions: keep us united in your love and tend to all our needs, be they material or spiritual. We beseech you, that we may be helped by the merit of the Spouse of your most holy Mother, so that what we cannot obtain by ourselves may be obtained by his intercession. Amen.

Day 3 – Joseph in Egypt

Theme: Love of the Eucharist

Opening Prayer

Remember, O most chaste spouse of the Virgin Mary, that never has it been known that anyone who asked for your help and sought your intercession was left unaided. Full of confidence in your power, I hasten to you, and beg your protection. Listen, O foster father of the Redeemer, to my humble prayer, and in your goodness hear and answer me. Amen.

Scripture

And Joseph stored up grain in great abundance, like the sand of the sea, until he ceased to measure it, for it could not be measured. (*Gn* 41:49)

Readings from St Bernardine of Siena and Pope St John Paul II

Let us consider this man Joseph in connection with the Universal Church of Christ. Is he not that elect and chosen one, through whom, and under whom Christ is orderly and honestly brought into the world? If, then, the Holy Universal Church be under a debt to the Virgin Mother (because through her the Church has been made to receive Christ), next to Mary the Church owes thanks and reverence to Joseph. He verily is the key which unlocked the treasures of the Church of the Old Testament, for in his person all the excellence of Patriarchs and Prophets comes to the completion of achievement, seeing that he alone enjoyed in this life the full fruition of what God has been pleased to promise aforetime to them. It is therefore with good reason that we see a type of him in that Patriarch Joseph who stored up corn for the people. But the second Joseph has a more excellent dignity than the first, seeing that the first gave to the Egyptians bread only for the body, but the second was, on behalf of all the elect, the watchful guardian of that Living Bread which came down from heaven, of which whosoever eats will never die.[4]

St Bernardine of Siena

In the Eucharistic Sacrifice, the Church venerates the memory of Mary the ever-Virgin Mother of God and the memory of St Joseph, because "he fed him whom the faithful must eat as the bread of eternal life".[5]

Pope St John Paul II

Reflection

The Joseph of whom we read in the Book of Genesis prefigures St Joseph. As the former was sold into slavery and taken to Egypt, so St Joseph brings the Holy Family to that place. The Old Testament Joseph became Pharoah's steward; the New Testament Joseph is given custody of the Son of God himself. The work of steward for the Pharaoh included guarding the vast royal stores of grain; St Joseph is guardian of the Bread of Life, born in the royal city of Bethlehem, a name that means 'House of Bread'. When we receive Holy Communion, we are entrusted with worthily receiving the Saviour of the world. May St Joseph inspire us to have greater love for this inestimable sacrament and instil in us trust when the path of life seems incomprehensible.

Prayer of St John Henry Newman

God has created me to do him some definite service; he has committed some work to me which he has not committed to another. I have my mission – I never may know it in this life, but I shall be told it in the next. Somehow I am necessary for his purposes, as necessary in my place as an Archangel in his – if, indeed, I fail, he can raise another, as he could make the stones children of Abraham. Yet I have a part in this great work; I am a link in a chain, a bond of connection between persons. He has not created me for naught. I shall do good, I shall do his work; I shall be an angel of peace, a preacher of truth in my own place, while not intending it, if I do but keep his commandments and serve him in my calling.

Therefore I will trust him. Whatever, wherever I am, I can never be thrown away. If I am in sickness, my sickness may serve him; in perplexity, my perplexity may serve him; if I am in sorrow, my sorrow may serve him. My sickness, or perplexity, or sorrow may be necessary causes of some great end, which is quite beyond us. He does nothing in vain; he may prolong my life, he may shorten it. He knows what he is about. He may take away my friends, he may throw me among strangers, he may make me feel desolate, make my spirits sink, hide the future from me – still he knows what he is about.

O Adonai, O Ruler of Israel, Thou that guidest Joseph like a flock, O Emmanuel, O Sapientia, I give myself to Thee. I trust Thee wholly. Thou art wiser than I – more loving to me than I myself. Deign to fulfil Thy high purposes in me whatever they be – work in and through me. I am born to serve Thee, to be Thine, to be Thy instrument. Let me be Thy blind instrument. I ask not to see – I ask not to know – I ask simply to be used.

Day 4 – David

Theme: A penitent heart

Opening Prayer

Remember, O most chaste spouse of the Virgin Mary, that never has it been known that anyone who asked for your help and sought your intercession was left unaided. Full of confidence in your power, I hasten to you, and beg your protection. Listen, O foster father of the Redeemer, to my humble prayer, and in your goodness hear and answer me. Amen.

Scripture

But that same night the word of the Lord came to Nathan, "Go and tell my servant David, 'Thus says the Lord:…When your days are fulfilled and you lie down with your fathers, I will raise up your offspring after you, who shall come from your body, and I will establish his kingdom. He shall build a house for my name, and I will establish the throne of his kingdom for ever. I will be to him a father, and he shall be to me a son.… And your house and your kingdom shall be made sure for ever before me. Your throne shall be established for ever.'" (*2 S* 7:4-5, 12-14, 16)

Readings from Pope Benedict XVI and St Francis de Sales

The figure of this great Saint, even though remaining somewhat hidden, is of fundamental importance in the history of salvation. Above all, as part of the tribe of Judah, he united Jesus to the Davidic lineage so that, fulfilling the promises regarding the Messiah, the Son of the Virgin Mary may truly be called the "son of David".[6]

Pope Benedict XVI

Oh, what a saint is the glorious St Joseph! He is not only a Patriarch, but the most distinguished among the Patriarchs. He is not merely a confessor, but far more than a confessor, for in him are included the dignity of the Bishop, the generosity of the martyr, the excellence of the other saints. St Joseph will obtain for us, if we repose confidence in him, an increase in every kind of virtue, but particularly in those which he possessed in a pre-eminent degree. These are a perfect purity of body and mind, humility, constancy, fortitude, and perseverance: virtues which will render us victorious over our enemies in this life, and enable us to obtain the grace of enjoying in the life to come those rewards which are prepared for the imitators of St Joseph.[7]

St Francis de Sales

Reflection

Despite God's overwhelming generosity to David and the promises God made to him, David grievously failed in "purity of body and mind, humility, constancy, fortitude, and perseverance". Yet, he was profoundly penitent and cried out to God for forgiveness and mercy: "Have mercy on me, O God, according to your merciful love; according to your great compassion, blot out my transgressions. Wash me completely from my iniquity, and cleanse me from my sin." (*Ps* 51(50):3-4). St Joseph, like his ancestor David, was not perfect and would have raised his heart and mind to God to beseech his mercy and healing love; with faith in the forgiveness of the Lord he would have praised him.

Prayer

I will sing for ever of your mercies, O LORD;
through all ages my mouth will proclaim your fidelity.
I have declared your mercy is established for ever;
your fidelity stands firm as the heavens.
"With my chosen one I have made a covenant;
I have sworn to David my servant:
I will establish your descendants for ever,
and set up your throne through all ages. […]

He will call out to me, You are my father,
my God, the rock of my salvation. [...]
I will keep my faithful love for him always;
with him my covenant shall last."

(*Ps* 89(88):2-5, 27, 29)

Day 5 – The Stock of Jesse

Theme: The gifts of the Holy Spirit

Opening Prayer

Remember, O most chaste spouse of the Virgin Mary, that never has it been known that anyone who asked for your help and sought your intercession was left unaided. Full of confidence in your power, I hasten to you, and beg your protection. Listen, O foster father of the Redeemer, to my humble prayer, and in your goodness hear and answer me. Amen.

Scripture

There shall come forth a shoot from the stump of Jesse, and a branch from his roots shall bear fruit. And the Spirit of the Lord shall rest upon him, the Spirit of wisdom and understanding, the Spirit of counsel and might, the Spirit of knowledge and the fear of the Lord. And his delight shall be in the fear of the Lord. (*Is* 11:1-3)

Readings from St Ephrem and Bl William Joseph Chaminade

Joseph is a paradise of delights. (*St Ephrem*)

How great his [St Joseph's] union with God, how sublime his gift of prayer, how wonderful the direction of the Holy Spirit! (*Bl William Joseph Chaminade*)[8]

Reflection

Pope Benedict XVI's baptismal name was Joseph. He reflected a number of times on aspects of his patron saint's life and mission, including, in 2021, linking Joseph to the prophecy of the tree of Jesse by proposing a new interpretation of the metaphorical depiction of Jesus's lineage in the Book of Isaiah. The then pope emeritus considered the image of this tree to be a 'silent reference' to St Joseph. Isaiah describes a sterile stump from which a new shoot will emerge that grows into a branch from which the Messiah will come. Traditionally, the branch has been imagined as a rose, symbolising the Blessed Virgin Mary. Pope Benedict, however, suggested that the name 'Nazareth' derived from the Babylonian word for a shoot – *nezer, nazar* – and was the only reference in the Old Testament to indicate the significance of that town for the Messiah. The dead stump of David's dynasty flourished as the tree of life, bestowing on the faithful the gifts of the Holy Spirit for which we pray.

Prayer

Holy Spirit, source of all grace and all love, it is through your action that St Joseph was so filled with attention for the divine plan and responded to God's will with such perfect fidelity. Since he intercedes for us and for the whole Church now, we pray through him. I ask you to inspire and to hear my prayer, so that there may be granted to me the favour entrusted to his intercession. Glory be to the Father…

Day 6 – St Joseph, the Man

Theme: Alive in the Spirit

Opening Prayer

Remember, O most chaste spouse of the Virgin Mary, that never has it been known that anyone who asked for your help and sought your intercession was left unaided. Full of confidence in your power, I hasten to you, and beg your protection. Listen, O foster father of the Redeemer, to my humble prayer, and in your goodness hear and answer me. Amen.

Scripture

Blessed indeed is the man
who follows not the counsel of the wicked,
nor stands in the path with sinners,
nor abides in the company of scorners,
but whose delight is the law of the LORD,
and who ponders his law day and night.
He is like a tree that is planted beside the
    flowing waters,
that yields its fruit in due season,
and whose leaves shall never fade;
and all that he does shall prosper. (*Ps* 1:1-3)

Reading from St Josemaría Escrivá

I don't agree with the traditional picture of St Joseph as an old man, even though it may have been prompted by a desire to emphasise the perpetual virginity of Mary. I see him as a strong young man, perhaps a few years older than Our Lady, but in the prime of his life and work.

You don't have to wait to be old or lifeless to practise the virtue of chastity. Purity comes from love; and the strength and joy of youth are no obstacle for noble love.[9]

Reflection

The Venerable Fulton Sheen is one of many to contradict the image that art has passed on to us of St Joseph, thanks to centuries of reliance on apocryphal writings. In his book *The World's First Love*, he wrote, "To make Joseph appear pure only because his flesh had aged is like glorifying a mountain stream that has dried." The archbishop instead presented St Joseph as strong and virile, handsome and chaste, athletic and disciplined – a man inflamed with love of God and of his wife, the Blessed Virgin Mary.

Lord, increase our love! "Give us life that we may call upon your name" (*Ps* 80:18).

Prayer of Pope St Pius X

O Glorious Saint Joseph, model of all those who are devoted to labour, obtain for me the grace to work in a spirit of penance for the expiation of my many sins; to work conscientiously, putting the call of duty above my natural inclinations; to work with thankfulness and joy, considering it an honour to employ and develop by means of labour the gifts received from God; to work with order, peace, moderation, and patience, never shrinking from weariness and trials; to work above all with purity of intention and detachment from self, keeping unceasingly before my eyes death and the account that I must give of time lost, talents unused, good omitted, and vain complacency in success, so fatal to the work of God.

All for Jesus, all through Mary, all after thy example, O Patriarch, Saint Joseph. Such shall be my watchword in life and in death. Amen.

Day 7 – The Silence of St Joseph

Theme: The fruit of silence

Opening Prayer

Remember, O most chaste spouse of the Virgin Mary, that never has it been known that anyone who asked for your help and sought your intercession was left unaided. Full of confidence in your power, I hasten to you, and beg your protection. Listen, O foster father of the Redeemer, to my humble prayer, and in your goodness hear and answer me. Amen.

Scripture

Behold, an angel of the Lord appeared to him in a dream, saying, "Joseph, son of David, do not fear to take Mary as your wife, for that which is conceived in her is from the Holy Spirit." (*Mt* 1:20)

Reading from Pope Benedict XVI

St Joseph's silence does not express an inner emptiness but, on the contrary, the fullness of the faith he bears in his heart and which guides his every thought and action.

It is a silence thanks to which Joseph, in unison with Mary, watches over the Word of God, known through the Sacred Scriptures, continuously comparing it with the events of the life of Jesus; a silence woven of constant prayer, a prayer of blessing of the Lord, of the adoration of his holy will and of unreserved entrustment to his providence.

It is no exaggeration to think that it was precisely from his "father" Joseph that Jesus learned – at the human level – that steadfast interiority which is a presupposition of authentic justice, the "superior justice" which he was one day to teach his disciples (cf. *Mt* 5:20).

Let us allow ourselves to be "filled" with St Joseph's silence! In a world that is often too noisy, that encourages neither recollection nor listening to God's voice, we are in such deep need of it.[10]

Reflection

Pope St Paul VI noted that "the Gospel does not record a single word from [St Joseph]; his language is silence". As Pope Francis declared, "silence enables true discernment, through attentive listening to the Spirit's 'sighs too deep for words' (*Rm* 8:26)". The example of St Joseph encourages us to rest from the noise that we can decide to surround ourselves with and to create pools of silence each day. He would have surely recognised the truth of the words of St Teresa of Calcutta: "The fruit of silence is prayer, the fruit of prayer is faith, the fruit of faith is love, the fruit of love is service and the fruit of service is peace."

Prayer

O St Joseph, in the silence of your heart, you welcomed the Word of God, communing in the fullness of your faith with the mysterious heavenly plan unfolding in your life. Guide us on the way of recollection, so that we may treasure silence as a place where we can hear the divine voice. Just as you listened to the angel, may we too find true peace in following God's will. Amen.

Day 8 – The Just Man

Theme: To examine my conscience

Opening Prayer

Remember, O most chaste spouse of the Virgin Mary, that never has it been known that anyone who asked for your help and sought your intercession was left unaided. Full of confidence in your power, I hasten to you, and beg your protection. Listen, O foster father of the Redeemer, to my humble prayer, and in your goodness hear and answer me. Amen.

Scripture

When Joseph woke from sleep, he did as the angel of the Lord commanded him: he took his wife. (*Mt* 1:24)

Reading from Pope St John Paul II

The word "*just*" evokes his moral rectitude, his sincere attachment to the practice of the law and his attitude of total openness to the will of the heavenly Father. Even in difficult and sometimes tragic moments, the humble carpenter of Nazareth never claimed for himself the right to dispute God's plan. *He awaited the call from on High* and in silence respected the mystery, letting himself be guided by the Lord. Once he received the mission, he fulfils it with *docile responsibility*. He listens attentively to the angel, when he is asked to take as his wife the Virgin of Nazareth (cf. *Mt* 1:18-25), in the flight into Egypt (cf. *Mt* 2:13-15) and in the return to Israel (cf. *Mt* 2:19-23). In few, but significant strokes, the Evangelists describe him as the caring guardian of Jesus, an attentive and faithful husband, who exercises his family authority in a constant attitude of service.

Nothing else is said about him in the Sacred Scriptures, but this silence contains the special style of his mission: a life lived in the greyness of everyday life, but with steadfast faith in Providence.[11]

Reflection

From the words of Pope St John Paul II, we can see that to live a "just" life is not only about our more significant acts but comes from a docility to the Holy Spirit that takes hold of each and every aspect of our life, even in "the greyness of everyday life". St Joseph steadfastly kept before his eyes and heart, and lived out, love of God and neighbour, the greatest of the commandments. He encourages us to examine our hearts and minds, and our actions as well. As St Pope Paul VI preached, "The Gospel describes St Joseph as a Just Man. No greater praise of virtue and no higher tribute to merit could be applied to a man".

Prayer of Bl Gennaro Maria Sarnelli C.S.S.R.

O chaste Spouse of Mary most holy, glorious St Joseph,
great was the trouble and anguish of your heart
when you were minded to put away privately your
inviolate Spouse, yet your joy was unspeakable when
the surpassing mystery of the Incarnation was made
known to you by the Angel!

By this sorrow and this joy, we beseech you to
comfort our souls, both now and in the sorrows of our
final hour, with the joy of a good life and a holy death
after the pattern of your own, in the arms of Jesus and
Mary. Amen.

Day 9 – Nurturer of the Son of God

Theme: Care of the divine life given to me

Opening Prayer

Remember, O most chaste spouse of the Virgin Mary, that never has it been known that anyone who asked for your help and sought your intercession was left unaided. Full of confidence in your power, I hasten to you, and beg your protection. Listen, O foster father of the Redeemer, to my humble prayer, and in your goodness hear and answer me. Amen.

Scripture

And while they were there, the time came for her to give birth. And she gave birth to her firstborn son and wrapped him in swaddling cloths and laid him in a manger, because there was no place for them in the inn. (*Lk* 2:6-7)

Reading from St Ephrem

Joseph caressed the Son as a Babe; he ministered to him as God. He rejoiced in him as in the Good One, and he was awe-struck at him as the Just One, greatly bewildered: "Who has given me the Son of the Most High to be a Son to me? I was jealous of your Mother, and I thought to put her away, and I knew not that in her womb was hidden a mighty treasure, that should suddenly enrich my poor estate. David the king sprang of my race, and wore the crown: and I have come to a very low estate, who instead of a king am a carpenter. Yet a crown has come to me, for in my bosom is the Lord of crowns!"[12]

Reflection

How St Joseph cared for the Child Jesus teaches me how I should care for the divine life that has been infused in me through Baptism. St Joseph battled against every danger that presented itself to his Holy Family. Am I so careful about the life of Christ within me, refusing to entertain thought, word or deed that might threaten this life with which I am entrusted?

Prayer of Bl Gennaro Maria Sarnelli C.S.S.R.

O most Blessed Patriarch, glorious St Joseph, who was chosen to be the foster father of the Word made flesh, your sorrow at seeing the Child Jesus born in such poverty was suddenly changed into heavenly exultation when you did hear the angelic hymn and beheld the glories of that resplendent night.

By this sorrow and this joy, we implore you to obtain for us the grace to pass over from life's pathway to hear the angelic songs of praise, and to rejoice in the shining splendour of celestial glory. Amen.

Day 10 – They Made Haste

Theme: Discerning what is important

Opening Prayer

Remember, O most chaste spouse of the Virgin Mary, that never has it been known that anyone who asked for your help and sought your intercession was left unaided. Full of confidence in your power, I hasten to you, and beg your protection. Listen, O foster father of the Redeemer, to my humble prayer, and in your goodness hear and answer me. Amen.

Scripture

And they went with haste and found Mary and Joseph, and the baby lying in a manger. (*Lk* 2:16)

Reading from St Francis de Sales

Oh, how divine was the union between Our Lady and the glorious St Joseph, a union which caused the Supreme Good, the Good of all goods, our Lord Himself, to belong to Joseph even as he belonged to Our Lady not by nature but by grace; which made him a sharer in all the possessions of his dear Spouse, and made him continually increase in perfection by his continual communications with her who possessed all virtues in so exalted a degree that no other creature, however pure and spotless, can attain to them!

Nevertheless, St Joseph was the one who made the nearest approach; and as a mirror when set before the rays of the sun reflects them perfectly, and another set before the first so vividly repeats them that it is scarcely possible to see which of the two immediately received them, even so Our Lady, like a most pure mirror, received the rays of the Sun of Justice, which conveyed into her soul all virtues and perfections; and St Joseph, like a second mirror, reflected them so perfectly, that he appeared to possess them in as sublime a degree as did the glorious Virgin herself.[13]

Reflection

The shepherds made haste to see the Lord Jesus lying in the manger. Some months earlier, Our Lady made haste to assist her pregnant cousin, Elizabeth. St Joseph would have made haste to find a safe and suitable lodging in which his wife could give birth.

Is there some good deed that I should do? Perhaps there is something truly important for others that I put off because I am driven by many lesser but seemingly urgent demands. May St Joseph's example help me to reflect upon my priorities that I may better reflect the divine light through my life.

Prayer

O St Joseph, you witnessed the miracle of birth, seeing the infant Jesus born of your most holy spouse, the Virgin Mary. With wonder and awe, you took into your arms the Saviour. With gratitude that only a parent can know, you glorified God for the birth of his Son, entrusted to your fatherly care.

Like you, St Joseph, I too give praise and glory to God for the children of the world. Each child's life is such a miraculous testimony of God's loving presence. May my heart be filled with grateful joy. Join me, dear St Joseph, in offering thanks to God for the gift of so many children.

What great trust and confidence God placed in you, St Joseph, by entrusting his only Son into your fatherly care. This inspires me to entrust the spiritual care and protection of all children into your caring and loving hands. Teach, guide, and support mothers and fathers and those entrusted to care for them so that they may fulfil their vocation to be worthy of the children entrusted to them. May all the children of God hear the message of Our Lord Jesus Christ and be open to the gift of faith in God: Father, Son and Holy Spirit. Amen.

Day 11 – The Naming of Jesus

Theme: The holy name

Opening Prayer

Remember, O most chaste spouse of the Virgin Mary, that never has it been known that anyone who asked for your help and sought your intercession was left unaided. Full of confidence in your power, I hasten to you, and beg your protection. Listen, O foster father of the Redeemer, to my humble prayer, and in your goodness hear and answer me. Amen.

Scripture

And at the end of eight days, when he was circumcised, he was called Jesus, the name given by the angel before he was conceived in the womb. (*Lk* 2:21)

Reading from Pope St John Paul II

A son's circumcision was the first religious obligation of a father, and with this ceremony (cf. *Lk* 2:21) Joseph exercised his right and duty with regard to Jesus.

The principle which holds that all the rites of the Old Testament are a shadow of the reality (cf. *Heb* 9:9f; 10:1) serves to explain why Jesus would accept them. As with all the other rites, circumcision too is "fulfilled" in Jesus. God's covenant with Abraham, of which circumcision was the sign (cf. *Gn* 17:13), reaches its full effect and perfect realisation in Jesus, who is the "yes" of all the ancient promises (cf. *2 Co* 1:20).

At the circumcision Joseph names the child "Jesus". This is the only name in which there is salvation (cf. *Ac* 4:12). Its significance had been revealed to Joseph at the moment of his "annunciation": "You shall call the child Jesus, for he will save his people from their sins" (cf. *Mt* 1:21). In conferring the name, Joseph declares his own legal fatherhood over Jesus, and in speaking the name he proclaims the child's mission as Saviour.[14]

Reflection

In obedience to the Law of Moses, the Child Jesus was circumcised on the eighth day after his birth. The ceremony, which would have taken place where the family were lodged, would not have been without pain for St Joseph and the Blessed Virgin Mary as they saw Jesus cry at the moment of circumcision and, for the first time, shed his Precious Blood. Yet this would also have been a solemn and joyful moment for St Joseph and Our Lady, with St Joseph, as instructed by the angel, pronouncing officially the name of the newborn child, the name that the Heavenly Father had deigned that his Son was to be called.

The name "Jesus" means Saviour and proclaims who Jesus is. God calls me by name, personally, and invites me to recognise in heart, mind and deed that he is the Saviour whom I need. Hence the power of the ancient "Jesus Prayer", with its words that can quietly be repeated again and again: "Lord Jesus Christ, Son of God, have mercy on me, a sinner."

Prayer of Bl Gennaro Maria Sarnelli C.S.S.R.

O glorious St Joseph, you faithfully obeyed the law of God, and your heart was pierced at the sight of the Precious Blood that was shed by the Infant Saviour during his Circumcision, but the Name of Jesus gave you new life and filled you with quiet joy.

By this sorrow and this joy, obtain for us the grace to be freed from all sin during life, and to die rejoicing, with the holy Name of Jesus in our hearts and on our lips. Amen.

Day 12 – The Light of Christ

Theme: To evangelise

Opening Prayer

Remember, O most chaste spouse of the Virgin Mary, that never has it been known that anyone who asked for your help and sought your intercession was left unaided. Full of confidence in your power, I hasten to you, and beg your protection. Listen, O foster father of the Redeemer, to my humble prayer, and in your goodness hear and answer me. Amen.

Scripture

And when the time came for their purification according to the Law of Moses, they brought him up to Jerusalem to present him to the Lord. (*Lk* 2:22)

Reading from St Sophronius

The Mother of God, the most pure Virgin, carried the true light in her arms and brought him to those who lay in darkness. We too should carry a light for all to see and reflect the radiance of the true light as we hasten to meet him.

The light has come and has shone upon a world enveloped in shadows; the Dayspring from on high has visited us and given light to those who lived in darkness. This, then, is our feast, and we join in procession with lighted candles to reveal the light that has shone upon us and the glory that is yet to come to us through him. So let us hasten all together to meet our God.[15]

Reflection

On the Feast of the Presentation of the Lord, all present at Mass carry lighted candles as they re-enact the entrance of the Lord into the Temple of Jerusalem. This symbolises our readiness to witness to the light of Christ in our own lives, not least in discerning how to speak to others of the gift that we have been given to share. To whom might I speak of the light of Christ?

Prayer

Almighty, ever-living God, we humbly beseech your Majesty that, as your only-begotten Son was presented in the temple in the substance of our flesh, so we also may, with purified hearts, be presented unto you. We make this prayer through our Lord Jesus Christ, your Son, who lives and reigns with you in the unity of the Holy Spirit, God, for ever and ever. Amen.

Day 13 – Gratitude

Theme: To discern what we ask for in prayer

Opening Prayer

Remember, O most chaste spouse of the Virgin Mary, that never has it been known that anyone who asked for your help and sought your intercession was left unaided. Full of confidence in your power, I hasten to you, and beg your protection. Listen, O foster father of the Redeemer, to my humble prayer, and in your goodness hear and answer me. Amen.

Scripture

And when the time came for their purification according to the Law of Moses, they brought him up to Jerusalem to present him to the Lord…and to offer a sacrifice according to what is said in the Law of the Lord, "a pair of turtle-doves, or two young pigeons". …And Simeon blessed them and said to Mary his mother, "Behold, this child is appointed for the fall and rising of many in Israel, and for a sign that is opposed (and a sword will pierce through your own soul also), so that thoughts from many hearts may be revealed."

(*Lk* 2:22, 24, 34-35)

Reading from St Bonaventure

He [St Joseph] lived content in his poverty.

Reflection

The offering of the Blessed Virgin and St Joseph was the offering of the poor – those who were richer would have presented a lamb and a pigeon or a dove. Yet, of course, the Lamb of God was presented that day, but the time of sacrifice was yet to come. The Holy Family would have been filled with gratitude to God for the gift of the Child Jesus and for all that they had. The Holy Family encourages us to nurture the gift of gratitude and to discern carefully that what we ask of God be according to his will.

Prayer of Bl Gennaro Maria Sarnelli C.S.S.R.

O most faithful Saint who shared the mysteries of our Redemption, glorious St Joseph, the prophecy of Simeon regarding the sufferings of Jesus and Mary caused you to shudder with mortal dread, but at the same time filled you with a blessed joy for the salvation and glorious resurrection which, he foretold, would be attained by countless souls.

By this sorrow and this joy, obtain for us that we may be among the number of those who, through the merits of Jesus and the intercession of Mary the Virgin Mother, are predestined to a glorious resurrection. Amen.

Day 14 – The Flight into Egypt

Theme: Compassion for those fleeing persecution

Opening Prayer

Remember, O most chaste spouse of the Virgin Mary, that never has it been known that anyone who asked for your help and sought your intercession was left unaided. Full of confidence in your power, I hasten to you, and beg your protection. Listen, O foster father of the Redeemer, to my humble prayer, and in your goodness hear and answer me. Amen.

Scripture

Now when they had departed, behold, an angel of the Lord appeared to Joseph in a dream and said, "Rise, take the child and his mother, and flee to Egypt, and remain there until I tell you, for Herod is about to search for the child, to destroy him." (*Mt* 2:13)

Reading from St Bernard

Who deserved to be called and to be regarded as the father of our Saviour? We may draw a parallel between him and the great Patriarch. As the first Joseph was by the envy of his brothers sold and sent into Egypt, the second Joseph fled into Egypt with Christ to escape the envy of Herod. The chaste Patriarch remained faithful to his master, despite the evil suggestions of his mistress. St Joseph, recognising in his wife the Virgin Mother of his Lord, guarded her with the utmost fidelity and chastity. To the Joseph of old was given interpretation of dreams, to the new Joseph a share in heavenly secrets.[16]

Reflection

Warned by the angel, the Holy Family fled to Egypt to escape from Herod's murderous hands. Could they have imagined what Herod was to unleash in Bethlehem – the slaughter of every male child under two years of age in Bethlehem and its region? For many, there are very clear warning signs that they and their families must flee their homes due to persecution and danger to their very lives, often due to religious persecution. Let us pray for these people and support, in prayer and practically, those forced to flee because of war, hatred or hunger. Let us support Christians who are being persecuted for their faith.

Prayer

Blessed Joseph, husband of Mary, be with us this day. You protected and cherished the Virgin; loving the Child Jesus as your Son, you rescued him from the danger of death. Defend the Church, the household of God, purchased by the Blood of Christ.

Guardian of the Holy Family, be with us in our trials. May your prayers obtain for us the strength to flee from error and wrestle with the powers of corruption so that in life we may grow in holiness and in death rejoice in the crown of victory. Amen.

Prayer of Pope Francis for Refugees

St Joseph,
you who experienced the suffering of those
    who must flee,
you who were forced to flee
to save the lives of those dearest to you,
protect all those who flee because of war,
    hatred, hunger.
Support them in their difficulties,
Strengthen them in hope, and let them find
    welcome and solidarity.
Guide their steps and open the hearts of those
    who can help them.
Amen.

Day 15 – In Egypt

Theme: Compassion in adversity

Opening Prayer

Remember, O most chaste spouse of the Virgin Mary, that never has it been known that anyone who asked for your help and sought your intercession was left unaided. Full of confidence in your power, I hasten to you, and beg your protection. Listen, O foster father of the Redeemer, to my humble prayer, and in your goodness hear and answer me. Amen.

Scripture

And he rose and took the child and his mother by night and departed to Egypt and remained there until the death of Herod. (*Mt* 2:14-15)

Reading from St Thomas Aquinas

Some Saints are privileged to extend to us their patronage with particular efficacy in certain needs, but not in others; but our holy patron St Joseph has the power to assist us in all cases, in every necessity, in every undertaking.[17]

Reflection

At different times of life and in different ways we all face adversity of some kind, as did the Holy Family. We are called to have compassion for those whom we know are suffering. If you are suffering, know the tender compassion of Jesus, Mary and Joseph for you.

> Even through Joseph's fears, God's will, his history and his plan were at work. Joseph, then, teaches us that faith in God includes believing he can work even through our fears, our frailties and our weaknesses. He also teaches us that we must never be afraid to let the Lord steer our course. At times, we want to be in complete control, yet God always sees the bigger picture.[18]

> Pope Francis

Prayer

We come to you, O Blessed Joseph, in our distress. Having sought the aid of your most blessed spouse, we now confidently implore your assistance also.

We humbly beg that, mindful of the affection which bound you to the Immaculate Virgin Mother of God, and of the fatherly love with which you cherished the Child Jesus, you will lovingly watch over the heritage which Jesus Christ purchased with his blood, and by your powerful intercession help us in our urgent need. Prudent guardian of the Holy Family, protect the chosen people of Jesus Christ; drive far from us, most loving father, all error and corrupting sin. From your place in heaven, most powerful one, graciously come to our aid in this conflict with the powers of darkness, and, as of old you delivered the Child Jesus from danger of death, so now defend the holy Church from the snares of the enemy and from all adversity.

Extend to each one of us your continual protection, that, led on by your example, and borne up by your strength, we may be able to live and die in holiness and obtain everlasting happiness in heaven. Amen.

Day 16 – Home

Theme: St Joseph at home

Opening Prayer

Remember, O most chaste spouse of the Virgin Mary, that never has it been known that anyone who asked for your help and sought your intercession was left unaided. Full of confidence in your power, I hasten to you, and beg your protection. Listen, O foster father of the Redeemer, to my humble prayer, and in your goodness hear and answer me. Amen.

Scripture

But when Herod died, behold, an angel of the Lord appeared in a dream to Joseph in Egypt, saying, "Rise, take the child and his mother and go to the land of Israel, for those who sought the child's life are dead." And he rose and took the child and his mother and went to the land of Israel. (*Mt* 2:19-21)

Reading from Pope Francis

Joseph saw Jesus grow daily "in wisdom and in stature and in favour with God and man" (*Lk* 2:52). As the Lord had done with Israel, so Joseph did with Jesus: he taught him to walk, taking him by the hand; he was for him like a father who raises an infant to his cheeks, bending down to him and feeding him (cf. *Ho* 11:3-4).

In Joseph, Jesus saw the tender love of God: "As a father has compassion for his children, so the Lord has compassion for those who fear him" (*Ps* 103:13).

In the synagogue, during the praying of the Psalms, Joseph would surely have heard often that the God of Israel is a God of tender love, who is good to all, whose "compassion is over all that he has made" (*Ps* 145:9).[19]

Reflection

As human beings, men and women with bodies animated by our souls, we need physical reminders of the supernatural. There is an old custom of keeping a statue of St Joseph in the kitchen, a place that is the heart of the home. Images of the saints are wonderful reminders that they are with us in our daily lives – watching over us, praying for us, encouraging us to live as they did.

Prayer

St Joseph, spouse of the Blessed Virgin Mary and foster father of the Son of God, in your authority, care and tenderness, you were a loving reflection of the Heavenly Father. You know the challenges with which all husbands and fathers are faced in the task of educating their children and providing for the needs of their families. Obtain for them the graces they need to raise their families according to the will of the Heavenly Father and to prepare them for eternity. Amen.

Day 17 – Daily Trials

Theme: Encouragement

Opening Prayer

Remember, O most chaste spouse of the Virgin Mary, that never has it been known that anyone who asked for your help and sought your intercession was left unaided. Full of confidence in your power, I hasten to you, and beg your protection. Listen, O foster father of the Redeemer, to my humble prayer, and in your goodness hear and answer me. Amen.

Scripture

And the child grew and became strong, filled with wisdom. And the favour of God was upon him.

(*Lk* 2:40)

Reading from St Thérèse of Lisieux

Good St Joseph! Oh! How I love him! I can see him planing, then drying his forehead from time to time. Oh! How I pity him! It seems to me their life was simple…What does me a lot of good when I think of the Holy Family is to imagine a life that was very ordinary. It wasn't everything that they have told us or imagined. For example, that the Child Jesus, after having formed some birds out of clay, breathed upon them and gave them life. Ah! No! Little Jesus didn't perform useless miracles like that, even to please his Mother. Why weren't they transported into Egypt by a miracle which would have been necessary and so easy for God. In the twinkling of an eye, they could have been brought there. No, everything in their life was done just as in our own.

How many troubles, disappointments! How many times did others make complaints to good St Joseph! How many times did they refuse to pay him for his work! Oh! How astonished we would be if we only knew how much they had to suffer![20]

Reflection

"Many are the trials of the just man", the Psalmist reflects. This is true for us all, and yet, at the time of such trials, there is a sense of isolation, that I alone am suffering. This sense of isolation is discouraging. A wise priest once opined that once we are discouraged, the devil sits back in his armchair, lights himself a cigar and pours himself a brandy. He need do nothing more. This cartoon image holds within it a truth. Our endurance of the trials of life is certainly individual, yet the human condition means that others will have been where we are. Dispirited, we are paralysed by fear or sadness or tiredness. May St Joseph help us put into perspective the troubles, disappointments and complaints that we suffer. He encourages us to turn to Jesus, who will console us, rekindle our hope and guide us. He encourages us to be forgiving and not to nurse grudges. "Good St Joseph!"

Prayer

O St Joseph, who as a father and guardian did most faithfully lead Christ Jesus in his boyhood and youth through all the ways of the human pilgrimage, I beseech you, assist me also as a companion and guide in the pilgrimage of my life and never permit me to stray from the path of God's commandments; in adversities, may you be a defence, in afflictions, a solace, until at last I come to the land of the living, where with you and Mary your most holy spouse, and all the saints, I may exult for ever in Jesus my God. Amen.

Day 18 – St Joseph the Worker

Theme: The value of work

Opening Prayer

Remember, O most chaste spouse of the Virgin Mary, that never has it been known that anyone who asked for your help and sought your intercession was left unaided. Full of confidence in your power, I hasten to you, and beg your protection. Listen, O foster father of the Redeemer, to my humble prayer, and in your goodness hear and answer me. Amen.

Scripture

And when they had performed everything according to the Law of the Lord, they returned into Galilee, to their own town of Nazareth. (*Lk* 2:39)

Reading from Pope St John Paul II

Human work, and especially manual labour, receives special prominence in the Gospel. Along with the humanity of the Son of God, work too has been taken up in the mystery of the Incarnation, and has also been redeemed in a special way. At the workbench where he plied his trade together with Jesus, Joseph brought human work closer to the mystery of the Redemption.

In the human growth of Jesus "in wisdom, age and grace," the virtue of industriousness played a notable role, since "work is a human good" which "transforms nature" and makes man "in a sense, more human."[21]

Reflection

At St Joseph's side, Our Lord Jesus Christ learned to be a carpenter and joined his foster father in his work, working as a carpenter for many years before he commenced his public ministry. Through our work, God invites us to take part in his work of creation and blesses us in that work whenever it is in accord with his creative plan. St Joseph is a saint who laboured his whole life long, someone who would have had many of the experiences that most of us have working with or for other people. He is also an intercessor for those who, through no fault of their own, have no work.

Prayer

We speak to you, O Blessed Joseph, our protector on earth, as one who knows the value of work and the response of our calling. We address you through your holy spouse, the Immaculate Virgin Mother of God, and knowing the fatherly affection with which you embraced Our Lord Jesus, ask that you may assist us in our needs, and strengthen us in our labours.

Be our watchful guardian in our work, our defender and strength against injustice and errors. As we look to your example and seek your assistance, support us in our every effort, that we may come to everlasting rest with you in the blessedness of heaven. Amen.

Day 19 – Finding the Boy Jesus in the Temple

Theme: Zeal

Opening Prayer

Remember, O most chaste spouse of the Virgin Mary, that never has it been known that anyone who asked for your help and sought your intercession was left unaided. Full of confidence in your power, I hasten to you, and beg your protection. Listen, O foster father of the Redeemer, to my humble prayer, and in your goodness hear and answer me. Amen.

Scripture

Behold, your father and I have been searching for you in great distress. (*Lk* 2:48)

Reading from St Aelred of Rievaulx

Christ's mother and foster father seek for their son in the greatest distress. At last they find him, and rebuke him, as St Luke tells us so vividly, and they take him back to Nazareth with them. And that is just what happens to holy men who have been given souls to look after, or who have been charged to preach the word of God. And I think that for them the Holy Spirit is foster father, while their mother is none other than Charity herself. Together they shower blessings and kindness on us who have souls in our care, encouraging us to journey on towards God, feeding and nourishing us with the twofold milk of love of God and of neighbour. Together they keep and sustain and refresh us as we strive for the things of God, just as Mary and Joseph supported the boy Jesus during the years of his youth at Nazareth.[22]

Reflection

I cannot imagine the feelings of the Blessed Virgin and St Joseph as they searched for their divine Son. In the psalms we are given the image of the deer yearning for running streams, along with the comment "so my soul is thirsting for you, my God". How true is this in my life? We cannot continually sustain a state of heightened fervour – in this life we walk by faith and it is sometimes a long, dark walk – but when our spiritual life seems arid and we no longer experience the sweetness of sensing the presence of God, he is urging us to seek him all the more, like the deer yearning for running streams, like Joseph and Mary searching for Jesus.

Prayer of Bl Gennaro Maria Sarnelli C.S.S.R.

O glorious St Joseph, pattern of all holiness, when you did lose, through no fault of your own, the Child Jesus, you sought him sorrowing for the space of three days, until with great joy you did find him again in the Temple, sitting in the midst of the doctors.

By this sorrow and this joy, we supplicate you, with our hearts upon our lips, to keep us from ever having the misfortune to lose Jesus through mortal sin; but if this supreme misfortune should befall us, grant that we may seek him with unceasing sorrow until we find him again, ready to show us his great mercy, especially at the hour of death; so that we may pass over to enjoy his presence in Heaven; and there, in company with you, may we sing the praises of his Divine mercy for ever. Amen.

Day 20 – The Holy Family

Theme: Faith seeking understanding

Opening Prayer

Remember, O most chaste spouse of the Virgin Mary, that never has it been known that anyone who asked for your help and sought your intercession was left unaided. Full of confidence in your power, I hasten to you, and beg your protection. Listen, O foster father of the Redeemer, to my humble prayer, and in your goodness hear and answer me. Amen.

Scripture

And he said to them, "Why were you looking for me? Did you not know that I must be in my Father's house?" And they did not understand the saying that he spoke to them. (*Lk* 2:49-50)

Reading from Pope Benedict XVI

When he was twelve years old, he stayed behind in the Temple and it took his parents all of three days to find him. With this act he made them understand that he "had to see to his Father's affairs", in other words, to the mission that God had entrusted to him (cf. *Lk* 2:41-52).

This Gospel episode reveals the most authentic and profound vocation of the family: that is, to accompany each of its members on the path of the discovery of God and of the plan that he has prepared for him or her.

Mary and Joseph taught Jesus primarily by their example: in his parents he came to know the full beauty of faith, of love for God and for his Law, as well as the demands of justice, which is totally fulfilled in love (cf. *Rm* 13:10).

From them he learned that it is necessary first of all to do God's will, and that the spiritual bond is worth more than the bond of kinship.

The Holy Family of Nazareth is truly the "prototype" of every Christian family which, united in the Sacrament of Marriage and nourished by the Word and the Eucharist, is called to carry out the wonderful vocation and mission of being the living cell not only of society but also of the Church, a sign and instrument of unity for the entire human race.

Let us now invoke for every family, especially families in difficulty, the protection of Mary Most Holy and of St Joseph. May they sustain such families so that they can resist the disintegrating forces of a certain contemporary culture which undermines the very foundations of the family institution.

May they help Christian families to be, in every part of the world, living images of God's love.[23]

Reflection

Jesus's explanation for his disappearance to St Joseph and Our Lady was all that they needed to hear – they knew that they did not need to understand. They had faith in God and trusted Jesus. They remind us of, as St Anselm put it, the importance of faith seeking understanding. We believe that Jesus is the Christ, the Way, the Truth and the Life, and we believe his promise that the Holy Spirit guides the Church. We believe the mystery of faith and do not expect to understand everything of the faith. We ask God to increase our faith and our understanding.

Prayer

O glorious St Joseph, to you God committed the care of his only begotten Son amid the many dangers of this world. We come to you and ask you to take under your special protection the children God has given us. Through holy baptism they became children of God and members of his holy Church. We consecrate them to you today, that through this consecration they may become your foster children. Guard them, guide their steps in life, form their hearts after the hearts of Jesus and Mary.

St Joseph, who felt the tribulation and worry of a parent when the child Jesus was lost, protect our dear children for time and eternity. May you be their father and counsellor. Let them, like Jesus, grow in age as well as in wisdom and grace before God and men. Preserve them from the corruption of this world, and give us the grace one day to be united with them in heaven for ever. Amen.

∽

Day 21 – The Humility of St Joseph

Theme: Humility

Opening Prayer

Remember, O most chaste spouse of the Virgin Mary, that never has it been known that anyone who asked for your help and sought your intercession was left unaided. Full of confidence in your power, I hasten to you, and beg your protection. Listen, O foster father of the Redeemer, to my humble prayer, and in your goodness hear and answer me. Amen.

Scripture

And he went down with them and came to Nazareth and was submissive to them. (*Lk* 2:51)

Reading from Origen

Joseph understood that Jesus was superior to him even as he submitted to him, and, knowing the superiority of his charge, he commanded him with respect and moderation. Everyone should reflect on this: frequently a lesser man is placed over people who are greater, and it happens at times that an inferior is more worthy than the one who appears to be set above him. If a person of greater dignity understands this, then he will not be puffed up with pride because of his higher rank; he will know that his inferior may well be superior to him, even as Jesus was subject to Joseph.[24]

Reflection

The Holy Family is a model of humility. It is certain that their humility was tangible to those in whom the Spirit was alive and active. Jesus, Mary and Joseph would have prayed the psalm "O LORD, my heart is not proud, nor haughty my eyes. I have not gone after things too great, nor marvels beyond me" (*Ps* 131:1), every word ringing true. In St Paul's Letter to the Philippians, we are admonished: "Do nothing from selfish ambition or conceit, but in humility count others more significant than yourselves. Let each of you look not only to his own interests, but also to the interests of others" (*Ph* 2:3-4).

Praises of St John Eudes

Hail, Joseph, image of God the Father,

Hail, Joseph, father of God the Son,

Hail, Joseph, temple of the Holy Spirit,

Hail, Joseph, beloved of the Most Holy Trinity,

Hail, Joseph, most faithful coadjutor of the
great counsel,

Hail, Joseph, most worthy Spouse of the Virgin Mary,

Hail, Joseph, father of all the faithful,

Hail, Joseph, guardian of all those who have
embraced virginity,

Hail, Joseph, faithful observer of holy silence,

Hail, Joseph, lover of holy poverty,
Hail, Joseph, model of meekness and patience,
Hail, Joseph, mirror of humility and obedience;
Blessed art you above all men,
Blessed your eyes, which have seen the things which
you hast seen,
Blessed your ears, which have heard the things which
you hast heard,
Blessed your hands, which have touched and handled
the Incarnate Word,
Blessed your arms, which have borne him who bears
all things,
Blessed your bosom, on which the Son of God
fondly rested,
Blessed your heart, inflamed with burning love,
Blessed be the Eternal Father, Who chose you,
Blessed be the Son, Who loved you,
Blessed be the Holy Spirit, Who sanctified you,
Blessed be Mary, your Spouse, who cherished you as
her Spouse and brother,
Blessed be the Angel who served you as a guardian,
And blessed for ever be all who love and bless you.
Amen.

Day 22 – The Angelic Man

Theme: My guardian angel

Opening Prayer

Remember, O most chaste spouse of the Virgin Mary, that never has it been known that anyone who asked for your help and sought your intercession was left unaided. Full of confidence in your power, I hasten to you, and beg your protection. Listen, O foster father of the Redeemer, to my humble prayer, and in your goodness hear and answer me. Amen.

Scripture

For you has he commanded his angels
to keep you in all your ways.
They shall bear you upon their hands,
lest you strike your foot against a stone. (*Ps* 91:11-12)

Reading from Jerónimo Gracián

The fact we are able to call God man, and subject to a woodworker, gives us courage yet to call this man, a carpenter, an angel on earth or in truth an angelic man.[25]

Reflection

Jerónimo Gracián, a sixteenth-century Carmelite friar, was the spiritual director of St Teresa of Avila. He contemplated St Joseph as "the Angelic man" because he saw in him the qualities of all the choirs of angels: most excellent in knowledge and love of God and most humble before him, in the execution of his will – making known his commands, commanding nature, fighting evil spirits, guiding nations, bringing his messages to men and women, and guiding individual souls. Being nearer to God, wrote Gracián, St Joseph surpassed all the angels. As such, St Joseph was not only attentive to the angels, as we know from Sacred Scripture, but the angels were, and are, highly attentive to him. In yet another way, he is a model to us all.

Prayer
Angel of God, my guardian dear,
to whom God's love commits me here,
ever this day be at my side,
to light and guard, to rule and guide. Amen.

Day 23 – The Shadow of St Joseph

Theme: Gentleness

Opening Prayer

Remember, O most chaste spouse of the Virgin Mary, that never has it been known that anyone who asked for your help and sought your intercession was left unaided. Full of confidence in your power, I hasten to you, and beg your protection. Listen, O foster father of the Redeemer, to my humble prayer, and in your goodness hear and answer me. Amen.

Scripture

Therefore, since we are surrounded by so great a cloud of witnesses, let us also lay aside every weight, and sin which clings so closely, and let us run with endurance the race that is set before us, looking to Jesus, the founder and perfecter of our faith, who for the joy that was set before him endured the cross, despising the shame, and is seated at the right hand of the throne of God. (*Heb* 12:1-2)

Reading from Pope Francis

The Polish writer Jan Dobraczyński, in his book *The Shadow of the Father*, tells the story of St Joseph's life in the form of a novel. He uses the evocative image of a shadow to define Joseph. In his relationship to Jesus,

Joseph was the earthly shadow of the heavenly Father: he watched over him and protected him, never leaving him to go his own way. We can think of Moses' words to Israel: "In the wilderness…you saw how the Lord your God carried you, just as one carries a child, all the way that you travelled" (*Dt* 1:31). In a similar way, Joseph acted as a father for his whole life. …

Jesus told us: "Learn from me, for I am gentle and lowly in heart" (*Mt* 11:29). The lives of the saints too are examples to be imitated. St Paul explicitly says this: "Be imitators of me!" (*1 Co* 4:16). By his eloquent silence, St Joseph says the same.

Before the example of so many holy men and women, St Augustine asked himself: "What they could do, can you not also do?" And so he drew closer to his definitive conversion, when he could exclaim: "Late have I loved you, Beauty ever ancient, ever new!"

We need only ask St Joseph for the grace of graces: our conversion.[26]

Reflection

As Jesus lived his earliest years under the protective shadow of St Joseph, so may we who consecrate ourselves to the saint look for his protection from all that would harm us. Among the virtues of the saint is gentleness, a virtue that Jesus Christ exemplified and undoubtedly saw in his foster father as he grew up. We can take Christ's teaching to heart: "Learn from me, for I am gentle and lowly in heart".

Prayer of Pope Francis
Hail, Guardian of the Redeemer,
Spouse of the Blessed Virgin Mary.
To you God entrusted his only Son;
in you Mary placed her trust;
with you Christ became man.
Blessed Joseph, to us too,
show yourself a father
and guide us in the path of life.
Obtain for us grace, mercy and courage,
and defend us from every evil. Amen.

Day 24 – Obedience to God's Word

Theme: Living in the love of God

Opening Prayer

Remember, O most chaste spouse of the Virgin Mary, that never has it been known that anyone who asked for your help and sought your intercession was left unaided. Full of confidence in your power, I hasten to you, and beg your protection. Listen, O foster father of the Redeemer, to my humble prayer, and in your goodness hear and answer me. Amen.

Scripture

But whoever keeps his word, in him truly the love of God is perfected. By this we may know that we are in him: whoever says he abides in him ought to walk in the same way in which he walked. (*1 Jn 2:5-6*)

Readings from Pope St John Paul II and Pope Benedict XVI

Joseph, in obedience to the Holy Spirit, found in the Holy Spirit the source of love. (*Pope St John Paul II*)[27]

Joseph was caught up at every moment by the mystery of the Incarnation. Not only physically, but in his heart as well, Joseph reveals to us the secret of a humanity which dwells in the presence of mystery and is open to that mystery at every moment of everyday life. In Joseph, faith is not separated from action. His faith had a decisive effect on his actions. Paradoxically, it was by acting, by carrying out his responsibilities, that he stepped aside and left God free to act, placing no obstacles in his way. Joseph is a "just man" (*Mt* 1:19) because his existence is "ad-justed" to the word of God.

The life of St Joseph, lived in obedience to God's word, is an eloquent sign for all the disciples of Jesus who seek the unity of the Church. His example helps us to understand that it is only by complete submission to the will of God that we become effective workers in the service of his plan to gather together all mankind into one family, one assembly, one "ecclesia".[28]

Pope Benedict XVI

Reflection

To hear God speaking to me and to adjust my life accordingly challenges me to create pools of silence in my daily life and to frequently raise up mind and heart to God to seek his guidance even in little matters. As St Thérèse of Lisieux said, "Holiness consists simply in doing God's will, and being just what God wants us to be."

Prayer

Glorious St Joseph, foster father and protector of Jesus Christ, to you I raise my heart and my hands to implore your powerful intercession. Please obtain for me from the kind Heart of Jesus the help and the graces necessary for my spiritual and temporal welfare. I ask particularly for the grace of a happy death and the special favour I now implore.

(*Make your petition here…*)

Guardian of the Word Incarnate, I feel animated with confidence that your prayers on my behalf will be graciously heard before the throne of God. O glorious St Joseph, through the love you bear for Jesus Christ, and for the glory of his name, hear my prayers and obtain my petitions. Amen.

Day 25 – Mary, His Spouse

Theme: Loving the Blessed Virgin Mary

Opening Prayer

Remember, O most chaste spouse of the Virgin Mary, that never has it been known that anyone who asked for your help and sought your intercession was left unaided. Full of confidence in your power, I hasten to you, and beg your protection. Listen, O foster father of the Redeemer, to my humble prayer, and in your goodness hear and answer me. Amen.

Scripture

His mother said to the servants, "Do whatever he tells you." (*Jn* 2:5)

Reading from Pope Benedict XVI

I…encourage you to look to St Joseph. When Mary received the visit of the angel at the Annunciation, she was already betrothed to Joseph. In addressing Mary personally, the Lord already closely associates Joseph to the mystery of the Incarnation. Joseph agreed to be part of the great events which God was beginning to bring about in the womb of his spouse. He took Mary into his home. He welcomed the mystery that was in Mary and the mystery that was Mary herself. He loved her with great respect, which is the mark of all authentic love. Joseph teaches us that it is possible to love without possessing. In contemplating Joseph, all men and women can, by God's grace, come to experience healing from their emotional wounds, if only they embrace the plan that God has begun to bring about in those close to him, just as Joseph entered into the work of redemption through Mary and as a result of what God had already done in her.[29]

Reflection

St Maximilian Kolbe once observed that no one could ever love the Blessed Virgin Mary too much because her Son, Jesus Christ, loves her even more and he is the one whom we desire to be like in all things. After Jesus, St Joseph loved his spouse, and in his prayers would have asked for his love to increase. To pray for our hearts to be expanded in love is something we all can do. Those who are married are called to love and respect each other and, if blessed with children, to lead them to God.

Prayer

Hail Mary, full of grace. The Lord is with thee. Blessed art thou amongst women, and blessed is the fruit of thy womb, Jesus. Holy Mary, Mother of God, pray for us sinners, now and at the hour of our death. Amen.

Day 26 – St Joseph Sleeps

Theme: Resting in the Lord

Opening Prayer

Remember, O most chaste spouse of the Virgin Mary, that never has it been known that anyone who asked for your help and sought your intercession was left unaided. Full of confidence in your power, I hasten to you, and beg your protection. Listen, O foster father of the Redeemer, to my humble prayer, and in your goodness hear and answer me. Amen.

Scripture

Come to me, all who labour and are heavy laden, and I will give you rest. Take my yoke upon you, and learn from me, for I am gentle and lowly in heart, and you will find rest for your souls. (*Mt* 11:28-29)

Reading from Pope Francis

The Scriptures seldom speak of St Joseph, but when they do, we often find him resting, as an angel reveals God's will to him in his dreams… Joseph's rest revealed God's will to him. In this moment of rest in the Lord, as we pause from our many daily obligations and activities, God is also speaking to us… Resting in the Lord. Rest is so necessary for the health of our minds and bodies, and often so difficult to achieve due to the many demands placed on us. But rest is also essential for our spiritual health, so that we can hear God's voice and understand what he asks of us. Joseph was chosen by God to be the foster father of Jesus and the husband of Mary. As Christians, you too are called, like Joseph, to make a home for Jesus. To make a home for Jesus! You make a home for him in your hearts, your families, your parishes and your communities.

I would also like to tell you something very personal. I have great love for St Joseph, because he is a man of silence and strength. On my table I have an image of St Joseph sleeping. Even when he is asleep, he is taking care of the Church! Yes! We know that he can do that. So when I have a problem, a difficulty, I write a little note and I put it underneath St Joseph, so that he can dream about it! In other words I tell him: pray for this problem![30]

Reflection

As a child, I remember how each school lesson began with a simple prayer. The teacher would say, "Let us remember that we are in the presence of God", the class responding, "Let us adore him": a few moments of silence followed. Sometimes our best prayer is as simple as this: pausing for a moment and lifting heart and mind to God.

Prayer

O Blessed St Joseph, who did accompany Jesus and Mary in all their journeys, and who has therefore merited to be called the patron of all travellers, accompany us in this journey through life. Be our guide and our protector; watch over us; preserve us from all accidents and dangers to soul and body; support us in our fatigue and aid us to sanctify it by offering it to God. Make us ever mindful that we are strangers, sojourners here below; that heaven is our true home; and help us to persevere on the straight road that leads there. We beseech you especially to protect and aid us in the last great voyage from time to eternity, so that, under your guidance, we may reach the realm of happiness and glory, there to repose eternally with you in the company of Jesus and Mary. Amen.

Day 27 – St Joseph, Patron of the Universal Church

Theme: St Joseph as protector and guardian

Opening Prayer

Remember, O most chaste spouse of the Virgin Mary, that never has it been known that anyone who asked for your help and sought your intercession was left unaided. Full of confidence in your power, I hasten to you, and beg your protection. Listen, O foster father of the Redeemer, to my humble prayer, and in your goodness hear and answer me. Amen.

Scripture

Who then is the faithful and wise servant, whom his master has set over his household, to give them their food at the proper time? Blessed is that servant whom his master will find so doing when he comes. Truly, I say to you, he will set him over all his possessions.

(Mt 24:45-47)

Readings from Bl Pope Pius IX and the Venerable Pope Pius XII

Him whom countless kings and prophets had desired to see, Joseph not only saw but conversed with, and embraced in paternal affection, and kissed. He most diligently reared him whom the faithful were to receive as the bread that came down from heaven whereby they might obtain eternal life. (*Bl Pope Pius IX*)[31]

If Joseph was so engaged, heart and soul, in protecting and providing for that little family at Nazareth, do you not think that now in heaven he is the same loving father and guardian of the whole Church, of all its members, as he was of its Head on earth?[32]

Venerable Pope Pius XII

Reflection

As St Joseph guided and protected his family, so he continues to care for the Church, the Mystical Body of Christ. This care is at the same time universal and particular: St Joseph wishes to guide our steps as we walk on the pilgrimage of life. His love for you is every bit as real as that love that he had and has for his Divine Son and the Mother of God.

Prayer

O Glorious St Joseph, you were chosen by God to be the foster father of Jesus, the most pure spouse of Mary, ever Virgin, and the head of the Holy Family. You have been chosen by Christ's Vicar as the heavenly Patron and Protector of the Church founded by Christ. Protect the Sovereign Pontiff and all bishops and priests united with him. Be the protector of all who labour for souls amid the trials and tribulations of this life; and grant that all peoples of the world may be docile to the Church without which there is no salvation.

Dear St Joseph, accept the offering I make to you. Be my father, protector, and guide in the way of salvation. Obtain for me purity of heart and a love for the spiritual life. After your example, let all my actions be directed to the greater glory of God, in union with the Divine Heart of Jesus, the Immaculate Heart of Mary, and your own paternal heart. Finally, pray for me that I may share in the peace and joy of your holy death. Amen.

☙

Day 28 – Almighty God

Theme: Take courage

Opening Prayer

Remember, O most chaste spouse of the Virgin Mary, that never has it been known that anyone who asked for your help and sought your intercession was left unaided. Full of confidence in your power, I hasten to you, and beg your protection. Listen, O foster father of the Redeemer, to my humble prayer, and in your goodness hear and answer me. Amen.

Scripture

I have said these things to you, that in me you may have peace. In the world you will have tribulation. But take heart; I have overcome the world. (*Jn* 16:33)

Reading from Pope Benedict XVI

Each and every one of us was thought, willed and loved by God. Each and every one of us has a role to play in the plan of God: Father, Son and Holy Spirit. If discouragement overwhelms you, think of the faith of Joseph; if anxiety has its grip on you, think of the hope of Joseph, that descendant of Abraham who hoped against hope; if exasperation or hatred seizes you, think of the love of Joseph, who was the first man to set eyes on the human face of God in the person of the

Infant conceived by the Holy Spirit in the womb of the Virgin Mary. Let us praise and thank Christ for having drawn so close to us, and for giving us Joseph as an example and model of love for him.[33]

Reflection

Towards the end of his life, a lady confessed to Blessed Dominic Barberi that she feared meeting the Lord and his judgement of her life when she died. Hearing this, a priest recalled, "the tears started in his eyes, and he cried out in his natural way, 'Oh, but how sweet to see for the first time the sacred Humanity of Jesus.'" That sight of the Lord who knows and understands each one of us is the sight of his face that we pray that we may know for eternity. For now, he is present to us veiled in the Sacraments of the Church to strengthen us in the joys and sorrows of our pilgrimage of life. St Thomas Aquinas's hymn, *Adoro te*, encourages us:

> Jesu, whom I look at shrouded here below,
>
> I beseech you send me what I long for so,
>
> Some day to gaze on you face to face in light
>
> And be blest for ever with your glory's sight.

Pope Benedict XVI once remarked, simply but with startling clarity, "God always wins."

Prayer of Pope Leo XIII

To you, O Blessed Joseph, we have recourse in our affliction. And having implored the help of your thrice-holy Spouse, we now, with hearts filled with confidence, earnestly beg you to take us also under your protection.

By that charity with which you were united to the Immaculate Virgin Mother of God, and by that fatherly love with which you cherished the Child Jesus, we beseech you and we humbly pray that you will look down graciously upon that inheritance which Jesus Christ purchased by his Blood, and will help us in our need by your power and strength.

Defend, O most watchful guardian of the Holy Family, the chosen off-spring of Jesus Christ. Keep from us, O most loving Father, all blight of error and corruption. Aid us from on high, most valiant defender, in this conflict with the powers of darkness. As you once rescued the Child Jesus from deadly peril, so now defend God's Holy Church from the snares of the enemy and from all adversity. Shield us ever under your patronage, that, following your example and strengthened by your help, we may live a holy life, die a happy death, and attain to everlasting bliss in Heaven. Amen.

Day 29 – St Joseph, Patron of a Happy Death

Theme: To live and die in the presence of Jesus, Mary and Joseph

Opening Prayer

Remember, O most chaste spouse of the Virgin Mary, that never has it been known that anyone who asked for your help and sought your intercession was left unaided. Full of confidence in your power, I hasten to you, and beg your protection. Listen, O foster father of the Redeemer, to my humble prayer, and in your goodness hear and answer me. Amen.

Scripture
The LORD is my shepherd;
there is nothing I shall want.
Fresh and green are the pastures
where he gives me repose.
Near restful waters he leads me;
he revives my soul.

He guides me along the right path,
for the sake of his name.
Though I should walk in the valley of the shadow
of death,
no evil would I fear, for you are with me.
Your crook and your staff will give me comfort.

You have prepared a table before me
in the sight of my foes.
My head you have anointed with oil;
my cup is overflowing.

Surely goodness and mercy shall follow me
all the days of my life.
In the LORD's own house shall I dwell
for length of days unending. (*Ps 22*)

Reading from St Alphonsus

Since we all must die, we should cherish a special
devotion to St Joseph, that he may obtain for us a
happy death. All Christians regard him as the advocate
of the dying who assists at the hour of death those who
honoured him during their life, and they do so for
three reasons:

First, because Jesus Christ loved him not only as a
friend, but as a father, and on this account his mediation
is far more efficacious than that of any other Saint.

Second, because St Joseph has obtained special
power against the evil spirits, who tempt us with
redoubled vigour at the hour of death.

Third, the assistance given St Joseph at his death by
Jesus and Mary obtained for him the right to secure a
holy and peaceful death for his servants. Hence, if they
invoke him at the hour of death he will not only help

them, but he will also obtain for them the assistance of Jesus and Mary.

Reflection

Traditionally it has been held that St Joseph died before the beginning of Jesus's earthly ministry – he certainly was dead by the time of the Saviour's Passion. That he died in the company of Jesus and Mary has been a piously held belief that has suggested to many that St Joseph experienced a "happy death". Each time we pray the "Hail Mary", we conclude with the words "pray for us sinners now and at the hour of our death". With the Lord calling us at that moment and Mary praying for us, we can hope that St Joseph may gather with his most intimate family beside us at our last hour, wherever and whenever that may be.

Prayer

O Blessed Joseph, you gave your last breath in the loving embrace of Jesus and Mary. When the seal of death shall close my life, come with Jesus and Mary to aid me. Obtain for me this solace for that hour – to die with their holy arms around me. Jesus, Mary and Joseph, I commend my soul, living and dying, into your sacred arms. Amen.

Day 30 – "I look forward to the resurrection of the dead and the life of the world to come"

Theme: Of you my heart has spoken,
"Seek his face."
It is your face, O LORD, that I seek. (*Ps* 27:8)

Opening Prayer

Remember, O most chaste spouse of the Virgin Mary, that never has it been known that anyone who asked for your help and sought your intercession was left unaided. Full of confidence in your power, I hasten to you, and beg your protection. Listen, O foster father of the Redeemer, to my humble prayer, and in your goodness hear and answer me. Amen.

Scripture

But the souls of the righteous are in the hand of God, and no torment will ever touch them. (*Ws* 3:1)

Reading and Reflection

The poem which follows contemplates Christ in the time between his death and resurrection, a time referred to in the words of the Apostles' Creed "He descended into hell". The poem speaks of the time between Christ dying in the flesh on Good Friday and his resurrection, depicting him appearing among the holy men and women who had died since the creation of the world. With his death and resurrection, Christ unlocked the gates of heaven for such as these of the past and of the generations to come.

"Limbo" by Sister Mary Ada, OSJ
The ancient grayness shifted
Suddenly and thinned
Like mist upon the moors
Before a wind.
An old, old prophet lifted
A shining face and said:
"He will be coming soon.
The Son of God is dead;
He died this afternoon."

A murmurous excitement stirred
All souls.
They wondered if they dreamed –
Save one old man who seemed
Not even to have heard.

And Moses, standing,
Hushed them all to ask
If any had a welcome song prepared.
If not, would David take the task?
And if they cared
Could not the three young children sing

The Benedicite, the canticle of praise
They made when God kept them from perishing
In the fiery blaze?

A breath of spring surprised them,
Stilling Moses' words.
No one could speak, remembering
The first fresh flowers,
The little singing birds.
Still others thought of fields new ploughed
Or apple trees
All blossom-boughed.
Or some, the way a dried bed fills
With water
Laughing down green hills.
The fisherfolk dreamed of the foam
On bright blue seas.
The one old man who had not stirred
Remembered home.

And there He was
Splendid as the morning sun and fair
As only God is fair.
And they, confused with joy,
Knelt to adore
Seeing that He wore
Five crimson stars

He never had before.

No canticle at all was sung
None toned a psalm, or raised a greeting song,
A silent man alone
Of all that throng
Found tongue –
Not any other.
Close to His heart
When the embrace was done,
Old Joseph said,
"How is Your Mother,
How is Your Mother, Son?"

Prayer

O Glorious St Joseph, behold I choose you today for my special patron in life and at the hour of my death. Preserve and increase in me the spirit of prayer and fervour in the service of God. Remove far from me every kind of sin; obtain for me that my death may not come upon me unawares, but that I may have time to confess my sins sacramentally and to bewail them with a most perfect understanding and a most sincere and perfect contrition, in order that I may breathe forth my soul into the hands of Jesus and Mary. Amen.

It is beyond doubt that Christ did not deny to Joseph in heaven that intimacy, respect, and high honour which he showed to him as to a father during his own human life, but rather completed and perfected it. Justifiably the words of the Lord should be applied to him, "Enter into the joy of your Lord." Although it is the joy of eternal happiness that comes into the heart of man, the Lord prefers to say to him "enter into joy". The mystical implication is that this joy is not just inside man, but surrounds him everywhere and absorbs him, as if he were plunged in an infinite abyss.

Therefore be mindful of us, blessed Joseph, and intercede for us with him whom men thought to be your son. Win for us the favour of the most Blessed Virgin your spouse, the mother of him who lives and reigns with the Holy Spirit through ages unending. Amen.[34]

St Bernardine of Siena

"Thirty Days" Prayer to St Joseph

Ever blessed and glorious Joseph, kind and loving father, and helpful friend of all in sorrow! You are the good father and protector of orphans, the defender of the defenceless, the patron of those in need and sorrow.

Look kindly on my request. My sins have drawn down on me the just displeasure of my God, and so I am surrounded with unhappiness. To you, loving guardian of the Family of Nazareth, do I go for help and protection. Listen, then, I beg you, with fatherly concern, to my earnest prayers, and obtain for me the favours I ask.

I ask it by the infinite mercy of the eternal Son of God, which moved him to take our nature and to be born into this world of sorrow.

I ask it by the weariness and suffering you endured when you found no shelter at the inn of Bethlehem for the Holy Virgin, nor a house where the Son of God could be born. Then, being everywhere refused, you had to allow the Queen of Heaven to give birth to the world's Redeemer in a cave.

I ask it by the loveliness and power of that sacred name Jesus, which you conferred on the adorable

I ask it by the painful torture you felt at the prophecy of holy Simeon, which declared the Child Jesus and his holy Mother future victims of our sins and of their great love for us.

I ask it through your sorrow and pain of soul when the angel declared to you that the life of the Child Jesus was sought by his enemies. From their evil plan, you had to flee with him and his Blessed Mother to Egypt.

I ask it by all the suffering, weariness, and labours of that long and dangerous journey.

I ask it by all your care to protect the Sacred Child and his Immaculate Mother during your second journey, when you were ordered to return to your own country.

I ask it by your peaceful life in Nazareth where you met with so many joys and sorrows. I ask it by your great distress when the adorable Child was lost to you and his mother for three days.

I ask it by your joy at finding him in the temple, and by the comfort you found at Nazareth, while living in the company of the Child Jesus.

I ask it by the wonderful submission he showed in his obedience to you.

I ask it by the perfect love and conformity you showed in accepting the Divine order to depart from this life, and from the company of Jesus and Mary.

I ask it by the joy which filled your soul, when the Redeemer of the world, triumphant over death and hell, entered into the possession of his kingdom and led you into it with special honours.

I ask it through Mary's glorious Assumption, and through that endless happiness you have with her in the presence of God. O good father! I beg you, by all your sufferings, sorrows, and joys, to hear me and obtain for me what I ask.

(*Here name your petitions or think of them.*)

Obtain for all those who have asked my prayers everything that is useful to them in the plan of God. Finally, my dear patron and father, be with me and all who are dear to me in our last moments, that we may eternally sing the praises of JESUS, MARY AND JOSEPH.

A blameless life, St Joseph, may we lead, by your kind patronage from danger freed. Amen!

Prayer of Consecration to St Joseph

O dearest St Joseph, I consecrate myself to your honour and give myself to you, that you mayest always be my father, my protector, and my guide in the way of salvation. Obtain for me a great purity of heart and a fervent love of the interior life. After your example, may I do all my actions for the greater glory of God, in union with the Divine Heart of Jesus and the Immaculate Heart of Mary! And do you, O Blessed St Joseph, pray for me that I may share in the peace and joy of your holy death. Amen.

Glory be to the Father,
and to the Son,
and to the Holy Spirit.

As it was in the beginning,
is now, and ever shall be,
world without end.
Amen!

Endnotes

1 Francis, General Audience, "Catechesis on St Joseph: 10", 2nd February 2022.

2 St John Henry Newman, *Meditations and Devotions*, pp. 309-310.

3 Benedict XVI, Angelus, 19th March 2006.

4 St Bernardine of Siena, Sermon 2, "On St Joseph".

5 St John Paul II, Apostolic Exhortation *Redemptoris custos*, 15th August 1989, 16, quoting the decree *Quemadmodum Deus*, Sacred Congregation of Rites (8th December 1870).

6 Benedict XVI, Angelus, 19th March 2006.

7 St Francis de Sales, Entretien XIX.

8 William J. Chaminade, *Marian Writings*, I, ed. J.B. Armbruster SM, p. 112.

9 St Josemaría Escrivá, *Christ is Passing By*, 40.

10 Benedict XVI, Angelus Address, 18th December 2005.

11 St John Paul II, General Audience, 19th March 2003.

12 St Ephrem, Hymn IV on the Nativity of Christ.

13 St Francis de Sales, Entretien XIX.

14 St John Paul II, Apostolic Exhortation *Redemptoris custos*, 15th August 1989, 11-12.

15 St Sophronius, Sermon.

16 St Bernard, Homily 2 on the "Missus Est".

[17] St Thomas Aquinas, *Commentary on the Sentences of Peter Lombard* (IV), 9, 45.

[18] Francis, *Patris corde*, 2.

[19] *Patris corde*, 2.

[20] St Thérèse of Lisieux, *Her Last Conversations*, from a conversation on 20th August 1897.

[21] *Redemptoris custos*, 22-23.

[22] St Aelred of Rievaulx, *On Jesus at Twelve Years Old*.

[23] Benedict XVI, Angelus, 31st December 2006.

[24] Origen, *Homily on St Luke*, XX, 5; Sources Chrétiennes, p. 287.

[25] Jerónimo Gracián, *Summary of the Excellencies of St Joseph*.

[26] *Patris corde*, 7.

[27] *Redemptoris custos*, 19.

[28] Benedict XVI, Address, 18th March 2009, Yaoundé.

[29] Benedict XVI, Address, 18th March 2009, Yaoundé.

[30] Francis, Address, 16th January 2015, Manila.

[31] Pius IX, *Quemadmodum Deus*, Sacred Congregation of Rites, 8th December 1870.

[32] Pius XII, *Acta Apostolicae Sedis*, vol. L (1958), n. 4, pp. 174-176.

[33] Benedict XVI, Homily, 19th March 2009, Yaoundé.

[34] St Bernardine of Siena, Sermon 2, "On St Joseph".